FEARFUL FERGUS LEARNS WATER SAFETY

By Sarah Chaires

Illustrated by Elizabeth Tortora

SEA STAR COOKIES

FEARFUL FERGUS
LEARNS WATER SAFETLY

Independently Published by Sarah Chaires

www.fergusthemastiff.com

ISBN: Paperback - 979-8-9925123-0-4

Ebook - 979-8-9925123-1-1

Author's Dedication:

*To my family & friends who
have supported and loved me
during my breast cancer journey!
Thank you!*

Fergus has never seen this much water!

The most water he's seen
in his ten weeks of puppyhood
is in his . . . silver bowl.
He loves to drench his sticky jowls
in the thirst-quenching water.
He can't wait to soak all his
sandy fur in the big pool of coolness.

Safe?

He puppy-ponders
what that word means.

SUDDENLY,
a shrieking noise blasts in the air.
Fergus whips his head around,
looking for the source.

The red noise maker is in the mouth
of a tanned, tall, sort of man-like boy
with red shorts and sunglasses.
Mom explains that the ear-piercing noise
is a "whistle," and the boy-like man
is a lifeguard.

Fergus puppy-ponders, *Lifeguard?*
Mom explains that lifeguards use the
whistle to help keep us safe.
They are trained to recognize
dangerous situations and
enforce rules that prevent

accidents,

injuries,

and

drownings.

The lifeguard proclaims:

"1. Always swim near a lifeguard.

2. Always wear your life jacket. It will keep your head above the water so you can breathe.

3. Only go in the water when your Water Watcher is ready to watch you."

Fergus springs into the air, soaring like a seagull.

KER-PLAT

He awkwardly cannonballs into the frigid water.

The water stings his eyes. All he sees is pitch darkness. He tries to take a deep breath but inhales only water.

Gulp · · ·
Gulp!

Suddenly, the life jacket propels him to the surface. Gasping for air. **FLOATING**.

He takes in his situation.

He now knows . . . he can't
breathe underwater
and the life jacket keeps him safe.

Moving his paws as he would on land,
Fergus tries to get to Mom.
But his nails are amiss with no floor to grip.
Even with his monstrous *splashes*,
his body is as stagnant as a slug.

Mom seems even further away now.

Fergus's **fear** sets in . . .
his **pounding** heart beats rapidly
from deep inside his chest.

Mom says, "Move your paws forward,

catch the water, scoop it,

and then push it past your belly."

Fergus tries to catch his breath,
panting and afraid.

Mom and the lifeguard **cheer**,
"You can do it.
You just need to try."

He needs to try to swim.
He needs to try to get to the wall.
Back to safety.
Back to Mom.

But he's so pooped!
He just bobs rhythmically.

Mom yells out, "Fergus, I have . . ."

Suddenly, a salty and sweet smell
captures his nostrils. **YUM!**

Alternating his paws foward, he **scoops** and pushes the water toward his belly.

Water *swishes* through his claws. Next paw, next scoop.

Next paw, next push.

His body starts to move—**slowly**,
like a tortoise. But he's so ᴛᴜᴄᴋᴇʀᴇᴅ out!
His trying halts . . . listless.
Yo-yoing up . . .
and down . . .
Alone . . . a solo shipwreck in the water.

Mom stacks a heap of sea star cookies,
like a school of fish on the pool deck.
Fergus contemplates
the risks and rewards of trying again.
Mouthful of deliciousness,
if I try?

Splish. Splash.

This time, the *scooping* and *pushing* move his body. **HUFFING** and **PUFFING** with each doggy paddle.

Now getting the rhythm, his body swims through the water like a speedy fish. Fergus finally reaches the wall. He **CONQUERED** his fear in the pool!

"I knew you could do it, Fergus!"
Mom cheers
"You just needed a life jacket and
sea star cookies to try!"

Mom wraps Fergus in a warm, cozy towel. *Water is fun*, Fergus thinks as he **chomps** on his **yummy** cookies, *but safety and swim lessons have to come first!*

Best Water Safety Practices To Keep Loved Ones Safe.

1. Keep four-sided fence or barrier around water.
2. Install alarms and locks on doors and gates near water.
3. Use surveillance cameras.
4. Drain bathtubs and put toilets seats down.
5. Have children (and adults) take swim lessons!
6. Stay within an arms reach of little ones.
7. Avoid substances while in the role of the Water Watcher.
8. Swim near a lifeguard.
9. Avoid water with rip currents.
10. Wear properly fitted U.S. Coast Guard approved life jackets!
11. Never swim alone.
12. Keep a charged phone nearby.
13. Avoid risk-taking behaviors.
14. Swim in designated swim areas.
15. Learn CPR and basic water rescue skills.

Sea Star Shortbread Cookies *by Chef Jason Lawless*

(Made for people, but safe for dogs)

Prep time: 20 minutes
Cook time: 12 minutes

Ingredients
1 cup softened butter
3/4 cups powdered sugar
1/2 tsp salt
1 tsp vanilla extract
1 3/4 cup flour
Sprinkles or sanding sugar

1) Preheat oven to 325 F. Mix the butter, sugar, salt, and vanilla until smooth in a large bowl using a rubber spatula or a free-standing mixer with a paddle attachment.

2) Slowly add the flour and mix to incorporate. The dough should be a little crumbly but come together when pressed.

3) Place the dough on a floured surface and roll it out with a rolling pin until about 1/4 inch thickness.

4) Using a starfish or large star cookie cutter, cut the shapes out and place them on a cookie sheet lined with parchment paper, about 1/2 inch apart

5) Roll out any extra dough and cut.

6) Add sprinkles to the cookies and lightly press with your fingers to ensure the sprinkles stick to the dough.

7) Refrigerate the cookies for 20-30 minutes. This will help the cookies keep their shape.

8) Bake for 10-12 minutes. Let cool for 5 minutes, then place it on a cooling rack to cool completely.

Enjoy!!

Signed by Fergus

www. fergusthemastiff.com

Fearful Fergus Learns To Try Series:
Pepperoni Cookies
Sea Star Cookies
More Cookies to Come!!

Authors Note:

This story is based on the true life events of Fergus, a real-life 250-pound English Mastiff.

His full American Kennel Club (AKC) title is:

Grand Champion HarvestHaze Fergus of The Sand Dunes.

He is a top-ranked AKC Conformation show dog in the United States.

About the Author

Sarah Chaires is a medical provider, Realtor and founder of a non-profit that provides educational opportunities for children in foster care. She and her husband are proud parents of three wonderful sons. Sarah is a Breast Cancer survivor. She and her family believe that the combination of self-confidence, love, and determination creates the ultimate superpower that catapults one to success . . . and it all starts with "YOU CAN DO IT!"

About the Illustrator

Elizabeth worked in advertising and toy design after graduating in graphic design from Parsons in NYC. After moving to NC and having two daughters and two dogs, she started a pet portrait business and loves Illustrating children's book, especially when there's animals involved. Elizabeth hopes the Fergus book series not only bring comfort and understanding, but also laughter and fun.

Contribution by

Executive Chef, Jason Lawless is a testament to this philosophy. Having previously worked and trained in some of the most discerning restaurants in the country, Lawless brings with him a passion for flavor and execution rooted in precision. He invites you to experience the theater, hospitality, and nourishment of the Mediterranean at Parizade. Lawless, hopes that you will love the fun Sea Star Cookie recipe that he created for this book!